LIVING IN THE WILD: PRIMATES

BONOBOS

Buffy Silverman

Heinemann
LIBRARY

Chicago, Illinois

www.capstonepub.com
Visit our website to find out
more information about
Heinemann-Raintree books.

To order:
☎ Phone 888-454-2279
🖥 Visit www.capstonepub.com
to browse our catalog and order online.

Edited by Abby Colich, Jilly Hunt, and Vaarunika
    Dharmapala
Designed by Victoria Allen
Picture research by Tracy Cummins
Original illustrations © Capstone Global Library
    Ltd 2012
Illustrations by Oxford Designers & Illustrators and
    HL Studios

Originated by Capstone Global Library Ltd
Printed and bound in China by CTPS

15 14 13 12 11
10 9 8 7 6 5 4 3 2 1

Library of Congress Cataloging-in-Publication Data
Silverman, Buffy.
  Bonobos / Buffy Silverman.—1st ed.
     p. cm.—(Living in the wild: primates)
  Includes bibliographical references and index.
  ISBN 978-1-4329-5861-9 (hb)—ISBN 978-1-4329-
5868-8 (pb) 1. Bonobo—Juvenile literature. I. Title.
  QL737.P96S547 2012
  599.8—dc22   2011012891

Acknowledgments
We would like to thank the following for permission
to reproduce photographs: Alamy pp. 14 (© A&J
Visage), 35 (© Photoshot Holdings Ltd); Corbis
pp. 38 (© Goran Tomasevic/Reuters), 39 (© Ian
Nichols/National Geographic), 41 (© Dominique
Derda/France 2); FLPA pp. 5 (Cyril Ruoso/Minden
Pictures), 20 (Cyril Ruoso), 26 (Frans Lanting),
30 (Frans Lanting), 31 (Cyril Ruoso), 44 (Frans
Lanting); Getty Images pp. 36 (Brent Stirton),
37 (Eric Feferberg); istockphoto p. 7
(© Michael Price); National Geographic pp. 8
(Frans Lanting), 15 (Cyril Ruoso/JH Editorial/
Minden Pictures), 22 (Cyril Ruoso/Minden Pictures);
National Geographic Stock p. 43 (Frans Lanting);
Photolibrary pp. 13 (Cyril Ruoso), 17 (Cyril Ruoso),
18 (Cyril Ruoso), 25 (Renaud Fulconis), 29
(Renaud Fulconis), 33 (Cyril Ruoso/Minden
Pictures); Photoshot pp. 19 (NPHA), 23 (NPHA);
Shutterstock pp. 6 (© worldswildlifewonders),
9 (© Kristof Degreef), 24 (© Uryadnikov Sergey).

Cover photograph of a young bonobo at Lola
Ya Bonobo Sanctuary, Democratic Republic of the
Congo, reproduced with permission of Photolibrary
(Renaud Fulconis).

Every effort has been made to contact copyright
holders of any material reproduced in this book.
Any omissions will be rectified in subsequent
printings if notice is given to the publisher.

Contents

Some words are shown in bold, **like this**. You can find out what they mean by looking in the glossary.

What Are Primates?

High-pitched screeches fill the forest. A group of bonobos chatters as the animals gather fruit from trees. While some of them eat, others extend their hands to beg for food. The bonobos share their meal.

Bonobos are primates. Primates are a group of **mammals** that includes monkeys, apes, and humans. Lemurs, lorises, bush babies, and tarsiers are primates, too. There are more than 350 different kinds of primates.

This map shows where in the world non-human primates live.

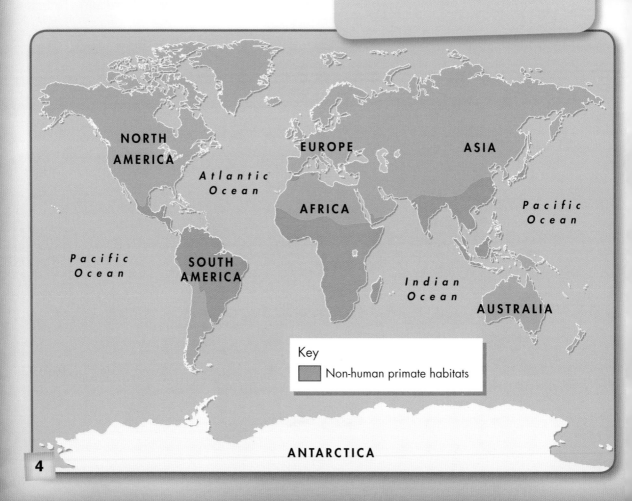

NORTH
AMERICA

EUROPE

ASIA

*Atlantic
Ocean*

AFRICA

*Pacific
Ocean*

*Pacific
Ocean*

SOUTH
AMERICA

*Indian
Ocean*

AUSTRALIA

Key

Non-human primate habitats

ANTARCTICA

Like all mammals, primates have fur and produce milk for their babies to drink. They give birth to live babies and care for their young. They breathe air and keep a constant, warm body temperature.

Living in trees

Many primates live in trees. Instead of paws, primates have hands and feet. Their five-fingered hands are useful for gripping tree branches. Touch the thumb of your right hand to the fingers of your right hand. It is easy, isn't it? You can do this because, like many primates, you have **opposable thumbs**.

Opposable thumbs allow primates to pick up objects. Primates can grab food with their hands and put it in their mouths. They can feel different objects with their sensitive fingertips. Most primates grip with their feet, too. Their big toes are like thumbs, helping them to climb and grasp.

These bonobos are playing with their keeper at a sanctuary in the Democratic Republic of the Congo, in Africa.

Hands and feet

Primates have other **adaptations** that allow them to make good use of their hands and feet. Instead of claws, primates have flat nails on their thumbs. Some have nails on all their fingers and toes. This allows them to pick up objects more easily than they could with clawed fingers.

Primates can twist their hands and feet in many directions. Two bones in their lower arms and legs allow them to do this. Many animals, such as dogs and cats, walk on their toes. Primates walk on flat feet. They can stand and walk upright.

This spider monkey uses its muscular tail like a fifth hand. It grabs fruits with its hands while it hangs by its tail.

Seeing the world

Primates have forward-facing eyes and excellent depth perception. This means that they can see three-dimensional (3–D) shapes and can judge distances. Primates know how far to reach for the next branch because of their depth perception. They depend more on their sense of sight than on their sense of smell. Because primates rely less on their sense of smell than other mammals, they have smaller, flattened noses.

Primates are intelligent, large-brained animals. They often live together in groups. They protect their young and teach them the skills they will need as adults. Young primates take a long time to grow up. While they are growing, they depend on their mothers for food and protection. Primates grow up slowly, but they live for a long time.

This silverback gorilla is **foraging** for food on the ground. He has found a tasty piece of bamboo.

What Are Bonobos?

It is hard not to be reminded of people when you watch bonobos. They pout, grin, and make funny faces. They tickle each other and laugh. They use facial expressions and hand gestures to communicate.

Along with chimpanzees, bonobos are our closest relatives. They share more than 98 percent of their **genes** with people.

This is a family of bonobos, including adults, young, and infants.

The unknown ape

Scientists once thought that bonobos were chimpanzees. However, although they do resemble each other, there are many differences. A bonobo's body is more slender. It has red lips and a darker face. Its head is smaller, with smaller ears, a thinner neck, and narrower shoulders. With their long legs, bonobos can stand more upright than chimps. Scientists think their posture resembles *Australopithecus*, an early human ancestor.

HAROLD COOLIDGE

In 1929 Harold Coolidge was studying a skull in a museum. It had been labeled as a young chimpanzee. Coolidge saw that the skull was from an adult, and that it was too small for a chimp. He realized that bonobos must be a separate **species**. In 1933 they were recognized as separate.

This mother and baby are chimpanzees. Can you see how they look different from the bonobos on page 8?

How Are Bonobos Classified?

When scientists **classify** living things, they place them in groups. Members of a group are related to one another and share certain characteristics. For example, you have more things in common with **mammals** than you do with animals in other groups, such as birds or fish.

Mammals are divided into many smaller groups. One of these groups is primates. Primates are further divided into six groups: lemurs; lorises, pottos, and bush babies; tarsiers; New World monkeys; Old World monkeys; and apes. Bonobos are a kind of ape.

Meet the apes

Within the apes, there are six more groups. These groups are gibbons, gorillas, chimpanzees, bonobos, humans, and orangutans. Gibbons belong to a group called the lesser apes. Gorillas, chimpanzees, bonobos, humans, and orangutans form the group known as the great apes. Orangutans split off from other great apes about 12 to 15 million years ago. Later, gorillas became a separate group. The group that was left eventually split off into three: humans, bonobos, and chimpanzees.

BONOBO RELATIVES

For thousands of years, people living in the forests of the Congo in Africa have respected and loved bonobos. They used to tell stories about how bonobos and people were once brothers.

About 5 to 8 million years ago, humans became a separate group. Bonobos and chimpanzees divided into two **species** more recently. Some scientists think this occurred between 690,000 and 900,000 years ago. Others say it may have been 1.8 million years ago. The Congo River in Africa, which formed about 1.5 million years ago, may have separated the two groups. The river still keeps bonobos and chimpanzees apart.

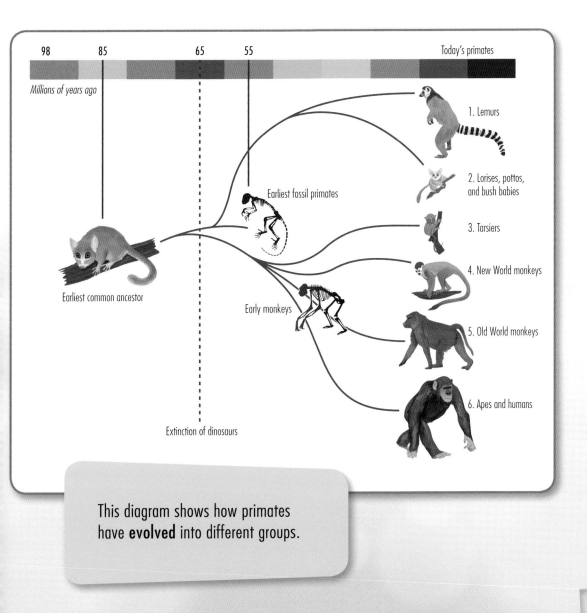

98   85   65   55   Today's primates

Millions of years ago

Earliest fossil primates

Earliest common ancestor

Early monkeys

Extinction of dinosaurs

1. Lemurs

2. Lorises, pottos, and bush babies

3. Tarsiers

4. New World monkeys

5. Old World monkeys

6. Apes and humans

This diagram shows how primates have **evolved** into different groups.

Where Do Bonobos Live?

A **habitat** is the place where an animal lives. Bonobos are found in the Democratic Republic of the Congo, in Africa, in a region called the Congo Basin. Three rivers border their habitat: the Congo River to the north and west; the Kasai River to the south; and the Lualaba River to the east. Many rivers run through the Basin, separating the various populations of bonobos.

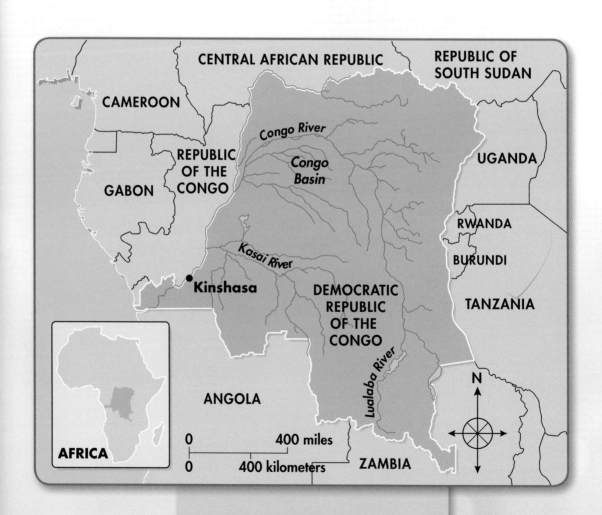

Bonobos live in the Congo Basin, south of the Congo River.

In the rain forest

The Congo Basin contains the second-largest **tropical rain forest** on Earth, and most of this region is swampy forest. It is warm and humid all year round. The average temperature is 79 to 82 °F (26 to 28 °C). Rain falls throughout the year, except during the dry season. There are also wetlands, grasslands, flooded forests, and farms. Bonobos look for food in all these places.

Leopards, forest elephants, okapi, and other rare animals also live in the Congo Basin. One thousand bird **species**, 400 **mammal** species, and 700 fish species inhabit the Congo Basin. There are probably more than 10,000 kinds of plants. Chimpanzees and gorillas live north of the Congo River. The forest here has more species than most places on Earth, but still fewer than other tropical rain forests.

Rain forests are kept relatively cool by shade from the trees.

What Adaptations Help Bonobos Survive?

Have you ever climbed to the top of a tree? You need strong arms and legs to pull yourself up. A strong grip helps you hold onto branches. You must use your balance and also plan the best route to reach the top.

Leaping and swinging

Bonobos not only climb trees. They also leap and swing across branches. They have many **adaptations** that help them survive in their forest **habitat**.

Bonobos have **opposable thumbs** as well as opposable big toes. They can grip branches and vines with their hands and feet. They can pick up small objects such as caterpillars and seeds. They can even pick fruit with their toes!

Here you can see a bonobo's opposable big toe.

Bonobos use all four limbs to climb up and down trees. They swing across long branches, reaching with one strong arm and then the other. Long, narrow shoulder blades allow their arms to swing with ease. They can travel long distances without touching the ground. Bonobos' slender bodies make them more acrobatic than chimpanzees in trees. Bonobos use their climbing skills to reach fruit high up in the treetops. Often they climb as high as 164 feet (50 meters) to pick ripe fruits.

This bonobo is swinging from branch to branch, while her infant clings to her stomach.

Tree travel

Bonobos need excellent balance to travel in trees. They cross thick branches on all fours, walking on their knuckles.

With their long legs, bonobos are also able to walk upright. Their long feet and thigh bones help them balance. More of their weight is in the lower part of their body. This means they can walk upright across wide branches, carrying food in their arms.

On the ground

Bonobos' strong legs allow them to leap from higher branches to lower ones. They leap and dive between trees. When frightened, bonobos jump down from the trees onto the ground. If there is danger beneath a tree, they scurry away on branches before leaping to the ground.

During the dry season, bonobos must travel farther to find food. Then they do most of their feeding and traveling on the ground. Bonobos move faster on the ground, as they run on all four limbs.

This bonobo is gathering sugarcane that has been cut by people. He can stand upright and grasp the cane, just like a human being.

Group living

Bonobos are social, which means they live in groups. This behavior is another adaptation that helps them to survive. Group members find food together and share it with each other. They care for and protect their young together, and they warn each other about danger. At night, they nest together in the safety of the trees.

Bonobos survive by living in groups and helping each other.

What Do Bonobos Eat?

A flying squirrel gnaws on fruits high up in a tree. A bonobo watches it silently from the ground. Suddenly, the bonobo leaps up the tree and grabs the squirrel. The tree, squirrel, and bonobo are all connected to each other in a relationship called a food chain.

Bonobos are omnivores, which means they eat both plants and animals. They eat many different foods, so they belong to many food chains. Many connected food chains add up to a food web. The more connections in a food web, the less affected it will be if one member of the web dies out.

These bonobos have spotted something delicious up in a tree.

Favorite foods

Fruit can make up more than half of a bonobo's diet. Bonobos will climb up very high trees to reach these fruits. When they find them, they eat the flesh and seeds.

Bonobos eat over 113 different plants. Leaves, bark, stems, roots, flowers, and seeds are all on the menu. They also eat mushrooms, honey, and soil. Animal food forms a smaller part of their diet. Bonobos catch insects, including caterpillars, bees, butterflies, and beetles. They dig for grubs, earthworms, millipedes, and termites. Bonobos capture small antelope, squirrels, and bats. Groups of bonobos may even hunt monkeys.

It is thought that leopards and pythons may hunt bonobos, but this has not actually been observed. People are the main predators of bonobos.

Bonobos scoop up water to drink from rivers and streams.

What Is a Bonobo's Life Cycle?

A young bonobo sits on a tree branch, watching his mother eat. He climbs onto her lap and tastes a bit of fruit. Like all **mammals**, a bonobo depends on its mother when it is young. It becomes more independent as it grows and matures.

The life cycle of an animal covers its birth to its death, as well as all the different stages in between. A bonobo's life cycle begins with mating. Female bonobos may mate with every male in their group. The father of an infant is not known. Female bonobos are pregnant for eight months before giving birth to a single baby.

This newborn bonobo is entirely dependent on its mother.

Baby bonobos

Bonobo mothers take good care of their babies. For the first three months of a baby's life, it never leaves its mother. The baby clings to the mother's belly and also drinks her milk.

By the time it is six months old, the baby starts to creep away. However, it does not go farther than about 3 feet (1 meter) from its mother. At around 10 months of age, a baby may crawl as far as 13 feet (4 meters) away. If it goes any farther, the mother brings the baby back to her side. At the age of one, a bonobo will begin to walk on four legs.

NEST BUILDING

Mother bonobos build nighttime nests that they share with their young. Every night, they climb up into the trees and build a new nest.

Bonobos will spend about four minutes building a nighttime nest. During the day, they also build day nests for the young to rest in. These will usually take less than a minute to construct.

A bonobo may build 19,000 nests during its life!

Growing up

For the first year of its life, a baby's only food is its mother's milk. It might put fruit in its mouth, but it does not actually eat it. As it grows a little older, the baby starts to try new foods. However, it will keep drinking its mother's milk until the age of four or five.

Around the age of two, a young bonobo begins to play. By three, a bonobo has learned to walk and climb almost as well as an adult. Even so, it stays near its mother. Instead of clinging to her front, it rides on her back.

A bonobo stays near its mother for the first four or five years of life. Like all great apes, bonobos have a long childhood.

Young bonobos love to play.

Leaving mom

Around the age of six or seven, female bonobos spend less and less time with their mothers. However, they continue to travel around in the same group as her, looking for food.

At eight years, females wander between different bonobo groups. They settle into a new group between the ages of 9 and 13. Male bonobos continue to grow until they are 14 to 16 years old. They stay in their mother's group even when they are fully grown.

A female bonobo has her first baby between the ages of 13 and 14. She gives birth every four to six years. During her lifetime, she will have five to six babies. A bonobo can live to be around 50 to 55.

This female bonobo is very old.

How Do Bonobos Behave?

Wild bonobos have not been studied as much as other apes, and many things about them are still a mystery to us. Most of what we know about them comes from observing them in zoos. Their behavior in the wild may be very different.

Looking for food

We do know that bonobos live together in groups. The size of a group ranges from 30 to 80 bonobos. Each day, the group divides up into smaller parties that travel together to look for food. These **foraging** parties can include just a few members or, when fruit is plentiful, 20 or more may band together. Mothers and their children will forage together, and sometimes males and females will, too.

This foraging party has found some fruit.

Sleeping

At night, the parties come together again. They choose the trees where they will spend the night. The forest becomes filled with their high-pitched squeals. They build new night nests, about 23 to 49 feet (7 to 15 meters) above the ground. They weave flexible branches together, then stamp them down. They fill the nest with leaves and twigs.

Bonobos groom each other, eat, and play in their nests while settling down for the night. When they fall asleep, bonobos look completely relaxed. They lie on their backs, holding onto a branch with just one foot. Baby bonobos sleep in a nest with their mothers. Adults sometimes sleep together, too. Bonobos are the only apes that share nests as adults.

This bonobo has settled down for the night in a new nest.

Crossing paths

During the day, one foraging party may cross paths with another from a different group. When two groups meet, there is a lot of excitement. Males may chase each other and bark. Females hug and groom each other. They use physical contact to reduce stress and conflict.

These females are grooming each other. Grooming helps them to create good relationships.

Females rule

Females within a group have strong bonds and cooperate well with each other. A band of females will sometimes keep males away from food. The sons of high-ranked females become leaders among the males. While females take care of the young, the males help protect them. When there is danger nearby, males will alert the others by barking.

Some scientists believe that bonobo societies are more peaceful than chimpanzee societies. Bonobos are more likely to share food and play with each other. Other scientists think that the differences between bonobos and chimpanzees are related to their **habitats**. Bonobos may fight less because they live in forests where food tends to be plentiful. It is likely that bonobo and chimpanzee groups have many different kinds of social interactions.

GOTTFRIED HOHMANN AND BARBARA FRUTH

Scientists Gottfried Hohmann and Barbara Fruth have been observing bonobos in the wild since 1989. They travel back and forth between Germany and Lomako Forest in the Congo. When they observe bonobos, they try to answer specific questions. For example, in their research about bonobo nests, they concluded that females build nests higher in the trees. They learned that females use nests for a longer time than males. Through careful research, they hope to get an accurate picture of bonobo society.

A DAY IN THE LIFE OF A BONOBO

The early morning sun peeks through the leaves in the **rain forest**. High up in a tree, a young bonobo awakes. He hears the high-pitched chatter of the bonobos around him. His mother has already risen from their shared nest. The young bonobo scratches and stretches.

He walks on all fours across a branch. He reaches for a small, hard fruit. As he chews, the fruit skin drops from the corners of his mouth. All around him, other bonobos eat.

Our bonobo follows his mother down, branch by branch, and drops to the ground. His mother joins a group of six other bonobos and they trek away. A few months earlier, he rode on his mother's back. Now, he keeps up on his own.

When the adults stop to eat, he stretches his open hand toward his mother. She hands him a tasty leaf. After he eats, he chases another young bonobo. They roll on the ground and play.

By the middle of the day, he is ready for a rest. His mother quickly builds a day nest. It is not as sturdy as their night nests, but it is fine for a nap. He drinks her milk and then dozes off.

Later in the afternoon, the bonobos go through the woods again. They stop to dig for termites. The youngster pops the wriggling insects into his mouth.

As the sun sets, the bonobo hears loud shrieks. The group has started to assemble. They are building nests for the night. The youngster follows his mother up the tree. After a busy day, he is ready for a rest.

A young bonobo stays close to his mother. He learns how to find food by watching and following her.

How Intelligent Are Bonobos?

When you were younger, an adult might have lain down and lifted you with his or her feet to play "airplane." Bonobos play the same game with their babies! Just as humans do, bonobos learn to cooperate and compete with one another through play.

Bonobos are among the most intelligent of non-human primates. Their societies are complex, so the young must learn many different social behaviors.

They play some of the same games that human children play. They chase and tickle each other and they tumble together. They climb up trees and jump to the ground. They make silly faces at each other.

Adult bonobos and their young play together, just as humans do.

Communication

Bonobos use facial expressions to tell other bonobos about their moods. These expressions can show whether they are feeling playful, relaxed, or aggressive. They use gentle pats to reassure each other. A begging gesture can be used to ask for support in a fight. The same gesture can be used to ask for food.

Gestures are often combined with sounds. Different sounds alert bonobos to food, threats, and the presence of others. Some scientists think that human communication may have begun with similar gestures.

After **foraging** in small groups, bonobo troops reunite at the end of the day. Scientists think they may exchange information about where to find food. We have much to learn about their communication.

These young bonobos are communicating by making funny faces!

Tool use in captivity

One of the main ways that scientists judge the intelligence of primates is by tool use. Tools such as spears and axes have helped human societies to hunt and build. Today, people use tools for almost every activity. Other primates have also learned to use tools to help them survive.

In zoos and in sanctuaries, bonobos are known to use tools. A bonobo will put a nut on a fallen log, pick up a rock, then use it to crack open the hard husk to reach the soft nut inside. Bonobos also use sticks to pull on objects that are out of reach. They make tools for scooping water and pulling termites out of mounds.

Tool use shows that bonobos can solve problems, such as how to crack open a nut.

Scientists wondered if bonobos could make sharp stone tools similar to the ones made by early humans. They showed Kanzi, a bonobo raised by humans, sharp flakes of stone that he could use to cut string. Kanzi eventually invented a way to make his own flakes.

Tool use in the wild

Unlike chimpanzees, bonobos have not been observed using tools to get food in the wild. This may be because food is plentiful, or because people have not studied bonobos enough to observe it. Bonobos do use tools for other purposes, however. They shoo away bees with leafy branches, and they bend shrubs to the ground so that they can sit on them like leafy cushions.

SUE SAVAGE-RUMBAUGH

Sue Savage-Rumbaugh studies ape-to-human communication at the Great Ape Trust in Des Moines, Iowa. She has known Kanzi, an adult bonobo, his entire life. When Kanzi was an infant, Sue tried to teach his mother to communicate with a keyboard. The keyboard had symbols that stood for different words. Kanzi's mother never mastered the keyboard. However, Kanzi picked up the language by himself. In addition to learning 200 symbols, Savage-Rumbaugh thinks Kanzi understands more than 3,000 words.

What Threats Do Bonobos Face?

Bonobos were once relatively safe, because few people went into the dense forests where they live. But over the past 30 years, the number of bonobos in the wild has dropped. Biologists think their populations will decline further over the next 50 years. They list bonobos as **endangered**. This means that bonobos face a high risk of **extinction**. No one is certain how many bonobos live in the wild. Scientists estimate that there are between 29,500 and 50,000. There may even be as few as 10,000 bonobos.

CLAUDINE ANDRÉ

When Claudine André volunteered at Kinshasa Zoo in 1993, an orphaned bonobo was brought there. André saved him, and soon more bonobos were brought to her. Some had been orphaned when their mothers were killed for bushmeat. André opened a sanctuary called Lola Ya Bonobo (Paradise for Bonobos). Today, 15,000 schoolchildren visit her sanctuary each year. They learn about the importance of protecting bonobos.

War and wildlife

Bonobos live only in the Democratic Republic of the Congo. The country experienced 10 years of civil war, ending in 2003. This war harmed people and bonobos. Over 4 million people died. Many people were left without their families and became very poor.

At one time, people in the Congo honored bonobos. They told a legend about a man who had fallen in the forest. He was saved by a bonobo that showed the man where to find food. Local people who told this story did not allow people to hunt bonobos. But during the war, some people began to hunt animals for their meat, known as bushmeat. Many bonobos were killed.

Smoked bonobo meat is sold at markets like this one.

Poaching

Poaching (illegal hunting) is the greatest threat to bonobos. As a result of the civil war, more people have guns. Poachers follow new roads into the **rain forests** in which bonobos live. Some poachers hunt and sell bushmeat as a way to survive. They also kill mother bonobos and sell their babies as pets.

Habitat loss

Habitat destruction also harms bonobos. Bonobos need large forests to find food. Illegal logging near bonobo reserves leaves bonobos without enough space. Foreign companies often run these tree-cutting operations. Their profits do not benefit local people, who still hunt bushmeat.

Logging threatens the forests where bonobos live.

Farming also destroys bonobos' habitats. People near rain forests often carry out slash-and-burn agriculture. They clear forests by cutting and burning trees. Mining also clears forests. Coltan is a mineral that is mined in the Congo. It is used in cell phones, DVD players, video game systems, and computers. Copper, uranium, gold, and diamonds are also mined. Pollution from mining harms people and bonobos.

Disease

Bonobos can catch many human diseases because we are so closely related. Logging roads bring more people into the forests. When people live near bonobos, the risk of spreading diseases increases. Ebola, a disease deadly to humans, now harms gorilla populations in the Congo. It could harm bonobos, too.

Mining pollutes the air and water. It harms habitats for people and bonobos.

How Can People Help Bonobos?

Bonobos are an important part of the **rain forest** in the Congo. They spread tree seeds by eating fruit. They help sustain the rain forest, which is an environment that people need.

People need bonobos

Along with chimpanzees, bonobos are our closest relatives. Studying their societies may reveal how human societies **evolved**. It may also show how we acquired language. People might benefit by understanding how bonobos resolve conflicts without war. For people to learn from and understand these creatures, we must protect bonobos and their **habitat**.

People care about bonobos in part because they remind us of ourselves. These feelings can lead people to get involved in protecting bonobos' habitats.

Understanding how bonobos resolve conflicts might one day help humans live more peacefully.

Taking action

Many people in the Congo and around the world are trying to protect bonobos and the rain forests where they live. In 2005 the Bonobo Peace Forest was created. It is a series of small forest reserves that are linked together. People who live in the reserves manage them. Local people work to protect their culture and the animals of the forest. They learn **sustainable** ways to use the forest resources. This means that they grow food and use forest products in ways that do not put rain forest plants and animals at risk.

LEARNING FROM BONOBOS

Chilean biologist Isabel Behncke Izquierdo studies bonobos in the wild. She thinks that there are three important things people can learn from bonobos: playfulness, social tolerance, and female closeness. Strong friendships between females seem to make bonobos more peaceful and tolerant.

Many people in the Congo work to protect bonobos and the rain forest.

Surveying bonobos

To decide how to protect bonobos, people must know where bonobos live. Many organizations are working to survey bonobo populations in the rain forest. Their goal is to estimate the number of bonobos and find where they feed and nest. They measure different characteristics of the forests where bonobos live. They look at the impact of people. Then they develop a plan to **conserve** the forest.

Some surveys are being done in the Congo's Salonga National Park. This is the largest **tropical** forest national park in Africa. It has been named a World Heritage Site, recognizing it as one of the world's most important natural places.

SANKURU NATURE RESERVE

In November 2007, the Democratic Republic of the Congo announced plans for a huge nature reserve. Called the Sankuru Nature Reserve, it is almost the size of Maryland. The creation of this nature reserve means that more than 10 percent of the land in the country is protected. The Sankuru Nature Reserve is home to bonobos, forest elephants, and other rare **mammals**. Helping people in Sankuru find ways to make a living other than the bushmeat trade is the first step for managing the new reserve.

Surveyors in Salonga National Park compare current bonobo populations with those before the civil war. Years of war have left Congolese people with few ways to survive. Many have turned to illegal hunting and logging. Park workers are trying to stop the poaching of bonobos and other **endangered** animals. They teach people the value of the rain forest and the animals that live there.

Guards patrol rivers surrounding Salonga National Park to stop poachers from entering the park.

What Does the Future Hold for Bonobos?

The future for bonobos is uncertain. Poaching and **habitat** destruction must be stopped for bonobos to survive. Because bonobos have only one baby at a time, illegal hunting has a huge impact on their numbers.

Bonobos and people

After years of civil war, many people who live in the Democratic Republic of the Congo are very poor. In order for bonobos to survive, people who live in and near their habitats also need help. Teaching people how to use forest resources without destroying them is critical. Congolese field biologists and park workers must be well trained so that they can lead their country's conservation efforts.

Because bonobos have not been known to science for as long as other apes, people know less about these fascinating creatures. Many people have never heard of bonobos. People in the Congo and around the world must learn about bonobos and the importance of protecting them.

Many groups are working to save bonobos and their habitats. You can help bonobos by teaching others about them. The more people know about bonobos, the more they will want to make sure that bonobos and their habitats survive.

Bonobos thrive in protected forests where they are not hunted.

SALLY JEWELL COXE

Sally Jewell Coxe is the president and cofounder of the Bonobo Conservation Initiative. For 10 years, her group has worked to **conserve** bonobos and their habitats. Together with Congolese communities and the government, she has helped create new protected areas for bonobos. The group's education programs promote traditional Congolese beliefs and culture. Respect for the animals of the **rain forest** is taught through Congolese stories and songs.

Bonobo Profile

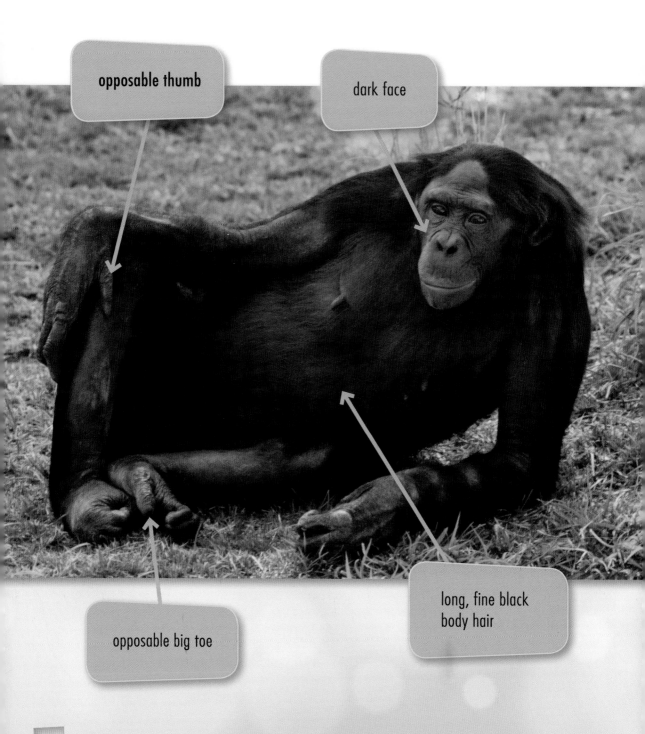

opposable thumb

dark face

opposable big toe

long, fine black body hair

Species: *Pan paniscus*

Weight: Adult males 99 pounds (45 kilograms); adult females 73 pounds (33 kilograms)

Height [from head to rump]: 28 to 35 inches (70 to 90 centimeters)

Habitat: Rain forests of the Congo Basin

Diet: Fruits, leaves, seeds, flowers, honey, eggs, soil, mushrooms, grubs, squirrel, antelope, monkeys

Number of young: One infant born after 8 months of pregnancy. Females will give birth every 4 to 6 years, after they have reached maturity at 13 to 14 years.

Life expectancy: 50 to 55 years

Glossary

adaptation body part or behavior of a living thing that helps it survive in a particular habitat

classify group living things together by their similarities and differences

conserve protect from harm or destruction

endangered living thing that is at risk of dying out

evolve change gradually over time

extinction when a type of living thing has died out

forage look for food over a wide area

gene information that is passed from parent to young and that determines species, as well as other characteristics

habitat natural environment of a living thing

mammal animal that has fur or hair, gives birth to live young, and feeds its young on milk from the mother

opposable thumb thumb that can face and touch the fingers on the same hand

rain forest forest with tall, thickly growing trees in an area with high rainfall

species group of similar living things that can mate with each other

sustainable able to be kept going over a long period of time

tropical regions of Earth around the equator

Find Out More

Books

de la Bedoyere, Camilla. *100 Things You Should Know About Monkeys and Apes*. New York: Barnes and Noble, 2008.

Moore, Heidi. *Protecting Food Chains: Rain Forest Food Chains*. Chicago: Heinemann Library, 2011.

Solway, Andrew. *Classifying Living Things: Classifying Mammals*. Chicago: Heinemann Library, 2009.

Websites

www.bonobokids.org
Visit this website to learn more about bonobos.

http://video.nationalgeographic.com/video/player/animals/mammals-animals/apes/chimp_bonobo_alphafemale.html
Watch a fascinating video about the role of female bonobos.

Organizations to contact

Bonobo Conservation Initiative
www.bonobo.org
This organization aims to help save the bonobo from extinction.

Friends of Bonobos
www.friendsofbonobos.org
This organization focuses on saving the bonobo.

World Wildlife Fund
www.wwf.org
WWF works to protect animals and nature.

Index